12
KISS HIM, NOT ME!
JUNKO

CONTENTS

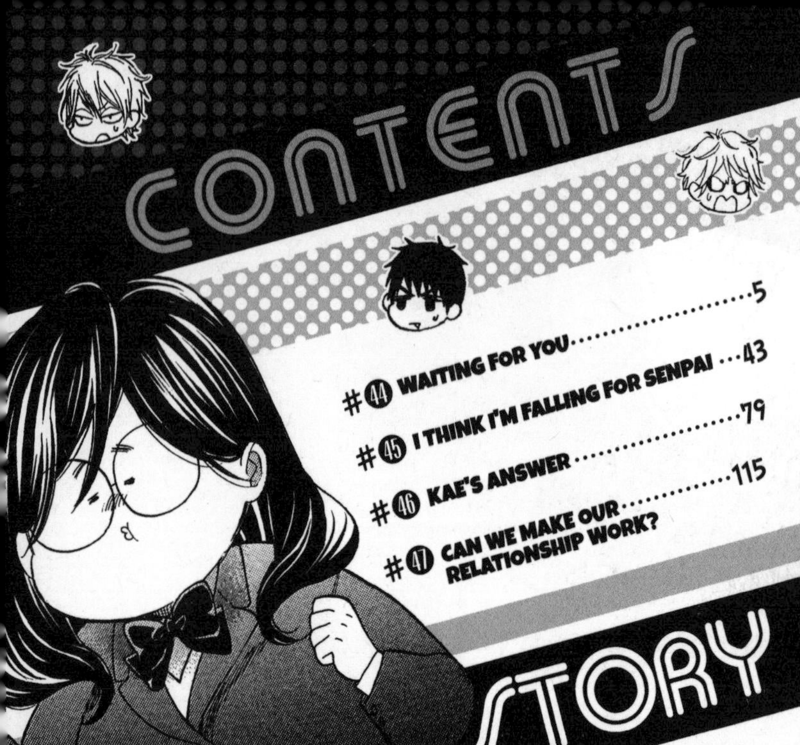

#44 WAITING FOR YOU 5
#45 I THINK I'M FALLING FOR SENPAI ...43
#46 KAE'S ANSWER 79
#47 CAN WE MAKE OUR RELATIONSHIP WORK? 115

STORY

...E REUNITES WITH HER CHILDHOOD FRIEND, **VOICE ACTOR MITSUBOSHI**. ...TH HIS MIND SOLELY ON **KAE**, **MITSUBOSHI'S** ACTIONS GRADUALLY ...ECOME MORE EXTREME! THINGS GET COMPLETELY OUT OF HAND AS ...E TAKES **KAE** WITH HIM ON HIS **NATIONAL TOUR**, THEN PROPOSES THAT SHE **MARRY** HIM, AND FORCES HER TO **PARTICIPATE IN THE WEDDING CEREMONY**!!

MUTSUMI AND THE GANG FIND IT STRANGE WHEN THEY CAN'T REACH **KAE**, AND AFTER FIGURING OUT HER AND MITSUBOSHI'S LOCATION, THEY TRY TO STOP **MITSUBOSHI'S** RAMPAGE. EVEN SO, **MUTSUMI** ENDS UP TRYING TO SAVE **MITSUBOSHI** FROM FALLING OFF OF A CLIFF, AND THE TWO END UP **FALLING** TOGETHER. AFTER THAT, **MUTSUMI** IS UNCONSCIOUS...!!

CHARACTER
THE MAIN CHARACTER— A FUJOSHI WITH WILD FANTASIES
A MUCH LOVED CHARACTER THAT YOU JUST CAN'T HATE. SHE'S OBSESSED WITH "AKANE-CHAN" FROM "KATCHU☆LOVE." ❤ (SHION HAS BEEN INDUCTED INTO THE HALL OF FAME)
SERINUMA KAE 芹沼花依
THE SPORTY CLASSMATE
ON THE SOCCER TEAM. THE POPULAR KID IN CLASS. HE'S SECRETLY TAKEN KAE TO A SPOT WITH A BEAUTIFUL NIGHT VIEW.
IGARASHI YUSUKE 五十嵐祐輔
THE FRIVOLOUS CLASSMATE
FORMERLY ON THE SOCCER TEAM. HE HAS A SMART MOUTH, BUT HE TELLS IT LIKE IT IS. HE STOLE A KISS FROM KAE WHILE HALF-ASLEEP.
NANASHIMA NOZOMU 七島希
THE SUB-CULTURE SENPAI
IN THE SAME HISTORY CLUB AS KAE. HE OFTEN SAYS CLUELESS THINGS. HE TREATS KAE THE SAME WAY AS HE DID IN THE BEGINNING.
MUTSUMI ASUMA 六見遊馬
THE HOT-N-COLD KOHAI
A MEMBER OF THE HEALTH COMMITTEE LIKE KAE. HIS GRANDFATHER IS NORWEGIAN. HE'S FALLEN INTO KAE'S CHEST TWICE.
SHINOMIYA HAYATO 四ノ宮隼人
NISHINA SHIMA 二科志麻
KAE'S CHILDHOOD FRIEND
HE WORKS AS THE VOICE ACTOR OF AKANE FROM THE ANIME "KATCHU☆ LOVE." SINCE LONG AGO, HE'S FELT SAFE HAVING KAE BY HIS SIDE.
THE HANDSOME FEMALE KOHAI
AND KAE'S FELLOW FUJOSHI FRIEND. A SUPER RICH YOUNG LADY. SHE WAS KAE'S FIRST KISS.
MITSUBOSHI TAKERU 三星建

KiSS HiM,
NOT ME!

#44 WAITING FOR YOU

MUTSUMI-SAN BROKE MITSU-BOSHI'S FALL...
...AND HIT HIS HEAD.
LUCKILY, IT WASN'T FATAL, AND HE DOESN'T NEED SURGERY...
BUT...

KiSS HiM, NOT ME!

HE HASN'T REGAINED CONSCIOUS-NESS YET...
...AND THEY DON'T KNOW IF HE WILL...
...!
NO!!
HUH ?!
DASH
HEY, KAE!!

BOOM
はぃっ
UH, EX-CUSE ME!!
EX-CUSE ME!!
SENPAI ...
WHERE IS MUTSUMI-SENPAI?!
WHAT?!
MUTSUMI-SENPAI ...?
OHH!
YOU MEAN MU-TSUMI-SAN?
ONLY FAMILY MEMBERS ARE ALLOWED TO SEE HIM NOW.
Kae !!
N...
NO!!

PLEASE!! SURELY YOU CAN MAKE AN EXCEP-TION!
I'M TRULY SORRY, BUT I CAN'T!
PLEASE !!
カララ…
RATTLE...
Conference Room
KAE, C'MON! LET'S HEAD BACK!!

?!
UH...
S...
SENSEI ?!
!
OH!!
YOU'RE... SERINUMA-SAN, RIGHT? I'M GLAD TO SEE YOU'VE COME TO!
SENSEI !!
Oh...
I'M NOT YOUR SENSEI ANY-MORE.
Ha ha!
I'VE SEEN HIM BEFORE...
You're kidding me...
HUH? YOU KNOW HIM?!
I THINK HE GOES TO THE SAME UNIVERSITY AS ME. SO HE'S PART OF MUTSUMI'S FAMILY, HUH...
WHOA, YOU'VE GOTTEN CHUBBY, HUH? HOW CUTE! YOU'RE LIKE A MEAT BUN!
UH, SO HE CAN TELL?!
?!
H...HE'S A MUTSUMI, ALL RIGHT!!
UH...
MORE IMPOR-TANTLY...

HOW'S SEN-PAI...?
WHERE IS HE ?!
WHEN WE TOLD HER WHAT HAPPENED TO MUTSUMI-SAN EARLIER... SHE BOLTED OUT OF HER ROOM TO FIND HIM...
KAE!!
SENSEI!!
Uh... I SEE.

I BEG YOU!!
PLEASE LET ME SEE SENPAI...
EVEN JUST A QUICK LOOK!!

ALL RIGHT...
COME THIS WAY.

Building No. 2
Asuma Mutsumi

RATTLE

? WHO ARE YOU ...?!
WOBBLE...

ピ
BEEP
ピ
BEEP
ピ
BEEP

...
SENPAI ...?

KA-ZUMA?
SHE'S ASUMA'S LOVE INTER-EST.
No big deal.
HUH?
UH, I SEE.

YOU WERE WITH HIM WHEN IT HAPPENED... RIGHT?
GASP
は
UH!
YES...
I...
I'M...

TOUCH...
...SORRY... SO SORRY...!!
IT'S ALL MY FAULT ...
IT'S 'CAUSE... I GOT SENPAI INVOLVED THAT... ALL OF THIS...!!
I HEARD THAT THIS HAPPENED BECAUSE HE WAS TRYING TO HELP A FRIEND.
IT'S NOT YOUR FAULT.
ASUMA IS JUST THAT KIND OF BOY...
CLENCH
...
PLEASE !!
LET ME LOOK AFTER SENPAI!!
GRAB
LET ME ATTEND TO HIM!! I'LL DO ANY-THING!!

TH... THAT'S VERY KIND OF YOU, BUT...
...WE COULDN'T VERY WELL MAKE ANOTHER PERSON'S DAUGHTER ...
GROVEL
I BEG YOU!!
UH...
WHY NOT? LET'S TAKE HER UP ON IT!
KA-ZUMA !!
Now, now! Get up!
I MEAN ...
HE MIGHT WAKE UP SOONER WITH A CLOSE FRIEND BY HIS SIDE.
WELL... IF YOUR PARENTS ARE FINE WITH IT,
CAN WE ASK THAT OF YOU?
THANK YOU!!

AND SO...
Huh?! You can't be serious...
Are you stupid ?!
I'm not leaving!
...AS WE WAITED FOR SENPAI'S CONDITION TO BECOME STABLE ENOUGH TO TRANSFER HIM TO A HOSPITAL IN TOKYO,
I STAYED BEHIND IN HOKKAIDO.
For God's sake! Then I'm staying behind, too!
Father came and went!
DAD
MAMA

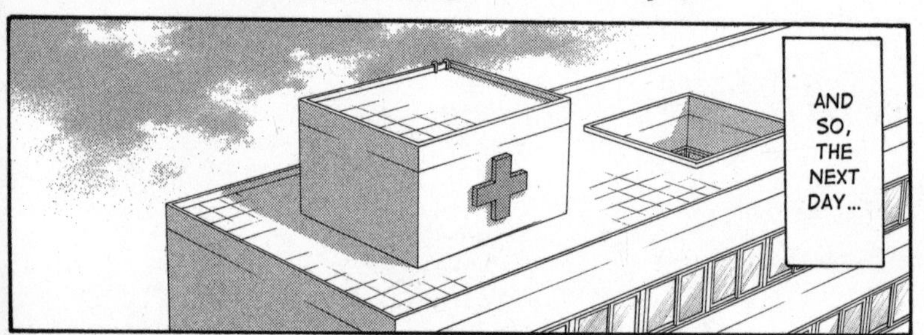
AND SO, THE NEXT DAY...

KNOCK
KNOCK

YES?
RATTLE
EX-CUSE ME!
COME ON, NOW.

RATTLE...
カラ…
...!!
TAH-KUN!!
ガタッ
CLATTER
...!
KAE-CH...
TMP
ハ…

GASP

I...
WOBBLE
DIDN'T MEAN...
...!

I'M SO SORRY ...
KAE-CHAN...

CLENCH
DON'T SAY THAT TO ME...
SAY THAT TO SENPAI ...
...WHEN HE WAKES UP.

IF THERE IS...
...ANYTHING I CAN DO...
ぱっ
FWIP
THERE IS, IN FACT, SOMETHING YOU SHOULD DO.
YOU STILL HAVE TO FINISH YOUR TOUR.
YOU HAVE FANS WAITING FOR YOU.
DON'T LET THEM DOWN, TOO.
THAT'S THE ONLY THING...
...YOU CAN DO FOR SENPAI NOW!!

PAT

BOW

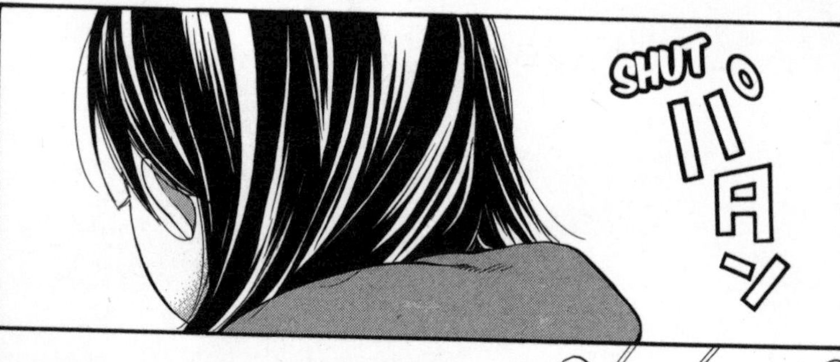
SHUT

SHE'S RIGHT. THE ONLY THING YOU CAN DO NOW...
I KNOW.
LET'S GO.
CLACK
CLACK

I'M SURPRISED SHE COULD SAY THAT AFTER ALL HE DID JUST YES-TERDAY...
THAT WAS THE RIGHT THING TO DO, RIGHT?
THAT'S WHAT YOU WOULD'VE SAID, RIGHT, SENPAI...?
GOOD-BYE...
TAH-KUN.

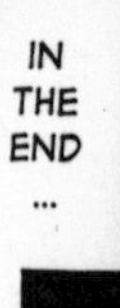
IN THE END ...
SHIMA-CHAN PULLED A FEW STRINGS, AND THE MATTER WAS SETTLED WITHOUT GOING PUBLIC...
This is power!

Hospital
SEVERAL DAYS LATER, MUTSUMI-SENPAI GOT TRANS-FERRED TO TOKYO.

And two weeks later...
SERINUMA-SENPAI IS ABSENT FROM SCHOOL AGAIN?
YEAH.
IT'S NO USE.
I DON'T THINK SHE'S GONNA BUDGE UNTIL HE WAKES UP.

AND SHE'S BEEN COOPED UP IN THERE THE WHOLE TIME...
SHINOMIYA, YOU WENT TO THE HOSPITAL YESTERDAY, RIGHT? HOW WERE THINGS?
Y... YES.

SHE LOOKED WELL, BUT...
I...I MEAN...
WELL, SHE'S ...
...GOTTEN QUITE THIN...

YEAH...
That makes sense.
AT THIS RATE, SHE'S GONNA END UP LOSING CONSCIOUS-NESS, TOO!
IS SHE EATING PROPER-LY?
I HOPE SENPAI IS OKAY ...
I...
...SAW HER.
HELLO!

HUH?! SHE'S NOT HERE?
OH!
THE GIRL WHO'S ALWAYS HERE? YOU'LL FIND HER ON THE ROOFTOP AROUND THIS TIME.
ガチャッ
KER-CHAK
SENPAI?
Are you here?
SEN— ?
GASP

EVERY-ONE!
PANT
PANT
PANT
PANT
LEND ME YOUR ENERGY!

AND, WELL ...
SHE WAS COLLECTING SPIRIT BALLS.
YIKES!!!
GASP

I HOPE SHE'S ALL RIGHT ...
TODAY'S MY TURN TO VISIT, SO I'LL TAKE SOME SNACKS WITH ME AND SEE HOW THINGS ARE GOING.

THAT'D BE GREAT.
WE'D LIKE TO COME, TOO, BUT IT'S NOT LIKE WE CAN ALL INTRUDE EVERY DAY.
YEAH, LEAVE IT TO ME.
THANKS!

Hospital
KNOCK
KNOCK
Asuma Mutsumi
RATTLE
EXCUSE ME.
SERI-NUMA-SAN, ARE YOU HERE ...?

HUH ... SHE'S SLEEP-ING...
No change with him, either.
TMP
TMP

すー...
ZZZ
すー...
ZZZ

SH...SHE REALLY HAS GOTTEN THINNER...
OR RATHER ... SHE'S WAST-ING AWAY.
CREAK...

ピ
BEEP
ピ
BEEP
ピ
BEEP

ピ
BEEP
ピ
BEEP
AT THE TIME ...
...I ONLY THOUGHT ABOUT STOPPING SERI-NUMA...
GRAB
DASH
...BUT MUTSUMI-SAN RAN TO SAVE MITSU-BOSHI...

...FOR SERI- NUMA- SAN...
GLANCE
YOU...
...REALLY ARE SOME- THING...

BUT...
MM...

JUMP
SEN- PAI!!
?!
JOLT

SEN-PAI!!
SERI-NUMA-SAN?! WHAT IS IT?!
FWIP
SEN-PAI WOKE UP!!
SEN-PAI'S AWAKE NOW!!
SEN-PAI!!
SERI-NUMA-SAN...
YOU WERE SLEEPING JUST NOW. DON'T YOU REMEMBER?
SO...
HUH?
HUH...?
NO!!
BUT EARLIER...!!
YOU WERE DREAMING!!
...
THUD

...
S...
AH!!
ぱっ
JOLT
Again?!
?!
IT'S SPIRIT BALL TIME!!!
I GOTTA COLLECT A BUNCH TODAY!!!

I'LL BE BACK!!!
DASH
S...SERI-NUMA-SAN!!!

WAIT !!
Hospital

FWIP
KER-
CHAK
EVERY-
ONE!
LEND
MUTSUMI-
SENPAI
A BIT
OF YOUR
POWER!!
SHE'S LOST
HER MIND!!
SHE HAS TO
REST, OR
SOMETHING
BAD WILL
HAPPEN!!
SERI-
NUMA-
SAN!!
YOU
NEED TO
REST A
LITTLE!!
NO!!
IF YOU
KEEP
THIS UP,
YOU'RE
GONNA
...
GASP
GRAB

BUT SENPAI WOKE UP EARLIER !!
H...
HE SMILED AT ME!!
THAT'S WHY...
THAT'S WHY I'M COLLECTING SPIRIT BALLS!
IF I GIVE IT ALL TO HIM...
...HE'LL COME BACK RIGHT AWAY!!

SOB
I HATE THIS!!
C... C'MON!
WAKE UP ALREADY!
I HATE THIS SO MUCH ...!!
SOB
I KNOW ...
WHIMPER
I KNOW ...
SERI-NUMA-SAN...
HOW MUCH LONGER ARE YOU GONNA MAKE SERINUMA-SAN CRY?!
HURRY UP AND COME BACK!
CLENCH...
BUT ...
MU-TSUMI-SAN!!

Hospital
RATTLE
HEY!
HOW'S HE HOLDIN' UP?
JOLT
OMINOUS
?!
OH! HI, SENSE... I MEAN, MUTSUMI-SENPAI'S OLDER BROTHER!!
YOUR MOTHER JUST LEFT!!

WH... WHAT ARE YOU DOING?
FLASH
WITH THIS HUMAN TRANS-MUTAT-ION CIRCLE, I'M SURE I'LL BE ABLE TO BRING BACK SENPAI'S SPIRIT!!
A WHAT CIRCLE...?!
ALL SET!! HERE I GO!!
E*!! LEND ME YOUR STRENGTH!!
SLAP

COME BACK, ASUMA MUTSUMI !!
BOOM
SILENCE
WHY DIDN'T IT WORK ?!!
PANT
PANT
FLAP
FLAP
FLAP
FLAP
FLAP
FMA
IS THE CIRCLE INCOMPLETE ?!
OR WAS IT BAD THAT I USED BOTH THE CIRCLE AND E*'S METHOD? NO, BUT I HAVEN'T ARRIVED AT THE GATE OF TRUTH, SO I CAN'T...
WH... WHY DON'T YOU CALL IT A DAY FOR NOW?
PLUS, THERE ARE MORE EFFECTIVE WAYS, DON'T YOU THINK ?
LIKE A PRINCESS'S KISS...
GASP
A PRINCE'S KISS WOULD WORK BETTER, WOULDN'T IT?!
NAW, I DON'T THINK THAT'D WORK ON ASUMA...
Though it might work on me.
INSTEAD OF THAT...
WHY DON'T YOU TALK TO HIM AND HOLD HIS HAND AND STUFF?
HE CAN APPARENTLY HEAR YOU.

HUH ...?
• • •
OH, SORRY, I GOTTA TAKE THIS.
VMMM
HELLO ?
SHUT
OHH ...

HOLDING HIS HAND ...

TOUCH...

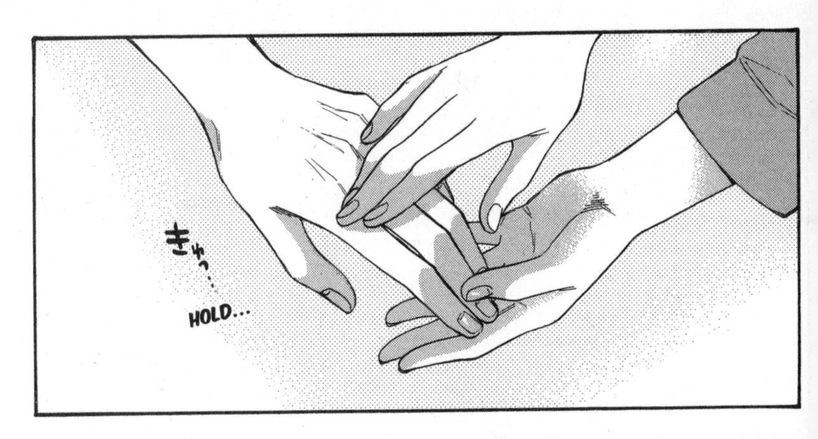
きゅっ…
HOLD...

CAN YOU ...
...HEAR MY VOICE?
SEN-PAI...
SENPAI ... YOUR HANDS ARE WARM...
AND SO BIG...

COME TO THINK OF IT ...
THE FIRST TIME WE HELD HANDS WAS WHEN WE ENTERED THAT CAVE, HUH?
YEAH... I DIDN'T KNOW YOU WERE AFRAID OF THE DARK,
YET YOU WANTED TO GO TO A PLACE LIKE THAT...
YOU'RE A STRANGE ONE, SENPAI...
AND WHEN I...
...SUDDENLY BECAME SKINNY, YOU RECOGNIZED ME RIGHT AWAY...
...AND YOU TREATED ME THE SAME WAY YOU ALWAYS DID, HUH?

YOU TOLD ME, "YOU'RE STILL YOU."
WHEN YOU SAID THAT...YOU MADE ME FEEL SO AT EASE.
SERI-NUMA-SAN, YOU TAUGHT ME...
...WHAT LOVE FEELS LIKE.
AND I REALLY ENJOYED OUR STROLL THROUGH TOWN...
WE STILL HAVE TO FULFILL THAT PROMISE TO VISIT ANOTHER PLACE, HUH?
AND...
...IN SPITE OF ALL MY INDECISION... YOU TOLD ME THAT YOU'D...
...CON-TINUE TO WAIT FOR ME...
YOU'VE ALWAYS ...
...BEEN BY MY SIDE,
EVEN WHEN I CAUSED YOU TROUBLE... YOU ALWAYS HELPED ME...
IT'S GONNA BE ALL RIGHT!!

WAIT
HERE!!

LIKE A PRINCESS'S KISS...

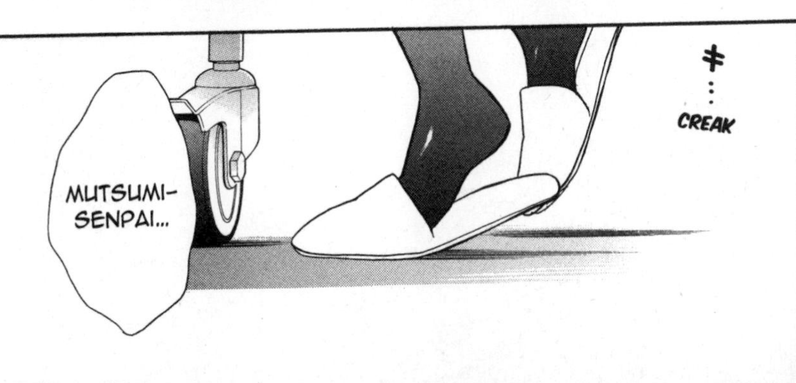

COME BACK...

#45 I THINK I'M FALLING FOR SENPAI...

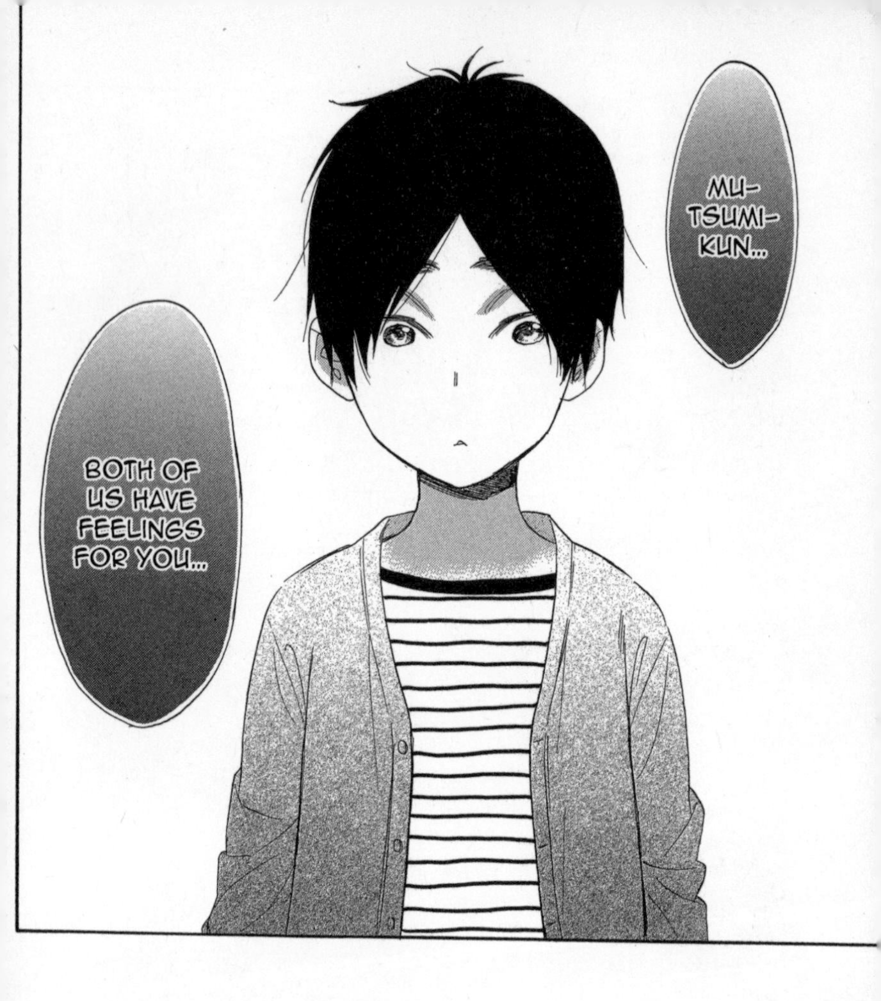

KiSS HiM, NOT ME!

WHICH OF US WILL YOU CHOOSE, MUTSUMI-KUN?!

UH...
I LIKE YOU BOTH.
You are both my classmates, after all.
SHOCK

WHAT KIND OF ANSWER IS THAT?! MUTSUMI-KUN, YOU IDIOT!!
HUFF
LET'S GO! LET'S GO!
HUFF
WHAT-EVER!

I...
I LIKE YOU...
WILL YOU GO OUT WITH ME?
HUH?
UH...
I GUESS, IF YOU WANT...
MUTSUMI-KUN...
YOU'D GO OUT WITH ANYONE, RIGHT?

WE'RE DONE.
GOOD-BYE.
HUH?
WHA...?

HMM. SO YOU GOT DUMPED, HUH?
I SEE, I SEE.
HA! HA! HA!
I WONDER WHAT WENT WRONG...
HMM?

I CAN TELL YOU WHY YOU GOT DUMPED, ASUMA...
YOU'RE TOO NICE.

I'M "TOO NICE" ?
WHAT'S WRONG WITH THAT?
I DON'T GET IT ...
O...
MURMUR
...KAY.
MURMUR
PRESS

THERE!
IT'LL BE GREAT IF THE CLUB GETS SOME NEW MEMBERS.
JOIN THE HISTORY CLUB!
HISTORY CLUB
NEW MEMBERS WELCOME

ALONE...

I GUESS I'M GONNA HAVE TO GO OUT AND RECRUIT PEOPLE.
Man, I'm terrible at this!
KNOCK
KNOCK

!
YES?
KNOCK

RAT
TLE
UM...
IS THIS THE HISTORY CLUB...?

UH,
YES!
WERE YOU INTERESTED IN JOINING, BY ANY CHANCE?
CLATTER
FIDGET FIDGET
UM...
DOES THIS CLUB COVER SENGOKU MILITARY COMMANDERS?
YES?
OF COURSE!
We can cover anything!
REALLY?!
BLUSH
......
UM, I'M KAE SERINUMA FROM CLASS 1-A.

MASAMUNE-SAMA IS MY FAVORITE! ♡
HE APPEARS IN THE GAME SENGOKU B*SARA WHICH MY OLDER BROTHER PLAYS, AND EVER SINCE I SAW HIM IN THAT GAME, I'VE BEEN THINKING ABOUT HIM DAY AND NIGHT! ♡
BLAH BLAH
BLAH BLAH
I SEE!
OH, AND I'M MUTSUMI, THE CLUB PRESIDENT.
WELCOME TO THE CLUB, SERINUMA-SAN!
THANK YOU!
LOOKING FORWARD TO IT!!
MUTSUMI-SENPAI!
UH, AND WHAT ABOUT THE OTHER MEMBERS...?
UH... WELL...
THE TRUTH IS, THE THIRD-YEAR STUDENTS GRADUATED, AND I'M THE ONLY ONE IN THE CLUB NOW.
BOOM
HUH?
AND NOT JUST THAT, WE NEED FOUR MEMBERS IN THE CLUB, OR IT'LL BE DISSOLVED...
WHAAA?!
BOOM

OH NO! W-WE CAN'T LET THAT HAPPEN!!
C'MON! WE GOTTA HURRY UP AND GO RECRUIT MORE MEMBERS!
YOU HAVE FLYERS, RIGHT?! LET'S COPY A BUNCH AND PASS THEM OUT!!
UH, OKAY.

CHATTER
CHATTER

HI! PLEASE CONSIDER JOINING THE HISTORY CLUB.
JOIN THE HISTORY CLUB
OH, I'VE ALREADY JOINED A CLUB.
So sorry.
SAME HERE.
OH...

UH, CAN WE HAVE A FLYER?
SQUEAL
SQUEAL
UH, SURE!
WHAT CLUB IS THIS?
So handsome!
IT'S THE HISTORY CLUB.

OH, ON SECOND THOUGHT...
NO THANKS!
BAIL
HEY!

THIS ISN'T LOOKING GOOD...
I WONDER IF SERI-NUMA-SAN IS DOING OKAY...

HEY, WHAT CLUB ARE YOU GONNA JOIN?
WHAT A PAIN! WHY ARE CLUBS MANDA-TORY?
I'D PREFER TO JOIN SOME-THING THAT'S NOT A SPORTS TEAM.
STAND
HEY.

YOU TWO ...
LOOM
...WOULD BE PERFECT FOR THE HISTORY CLUB!!

STRAFE
I... IT'S OKAY ...
NOW, NOW, NOW!
STRAFE
W... WE'RE IN A HURRY !!
NOW, NOW, NOW!

C'MON! LET'S TALK ABOUT THIS IN THE CLUBROOM!!
CREEP...
CREEP...
H-HEEEEK! STOP COMING SO CLOSE!!
AHHHHH!
NOW, NOW, NOW!!

SIGH. THIS DIDN'T GO WELL AT ALL...
PLOD
I GOTTA COME UP WITH SOME KINDA PLAN...
PLOD
HM?
CHATTER
CHATTER

RATTLE

HEY! DO YOU KNOW "CASTLE GUARD," TOO?! LET'S HAVE A MATCH NEXT TIME!!
CHATTER
CHATTER
WHAT? YOU KNOW ABOUT THAT GAME?! YEAH, WE SHOULD TOTALLY PLAY!
YOU LOOK LIKE YOU'D BE GOOD.

OH, SENPAI!
THESE TWO SAID THEY'RE GONNA JOIN THE CLUB!
RIGHT?
UH, RIGHT.
Thanks...?
NOW WE HAVE ENOUGH MEMBERS FOR OUR CLUB, RIGHT?!
THANK GOD!!
OKAY, YOU PUNKS! LET'S PARTY!!
YEAH!!
HEH, HEH.
AMAZ-ING...
SHE'S KINDA...

...LIKE A BALL OF SUNSHINE.
YOU'RE THE ONLY ONE WHO UNDER-STANDS ME, SENPAI.
THANK YOU!

HER APPEARANCE CHANGED A LITTLE ...
...AND MORE PEOPLE SURROUNDED HER.

I HAVE SO MUCH FUN BEING WITH ALL OF THEM...
THESE GUYS...
...WHO I WOULD'VE NEVER MET WERE IT NOT FOR HER.

I...
AS WELL AS NANA AND SHINOMIYA...
YEAH.
I LIKE HER JUST LIKE THEY DO... THAT'S WHY I'M HERE.
YEAH.

I KNOW THAT.
ONCE YOU GET TO KNOW HER, IT'S ONLY NATURAL TO LIKE HER.
THE SAME...
I...
...GOES FOR YOU YOU, RIGHT?

HOW DO YOU FEEL ABOUT SERINUMA-SAN?
HUH?
TO ME ...
TO ME ...
SHE IS...

ドキン
BADUMP
YOU'D GO OUT WITH ANYONE, RIGHT?
ドキン
BADUMP
YOU GOT DUMPED 'CAUSE YOU'RE TOO NICE.
SHE'S ...
...A GIRL NO ONE ELSE CAN RE-PLACE.
A SPECIAL GIRL...
SENPAI ...
ドキン
BADUMP

SHE'S ONE OF A KIND.
SENPAI...
AREN'T YOU HUNGRY?
GRIN
HUNGRY ...?
GASP
WHA ?!
HUH?
TA-DAH
HERE!
I'VE PREP-ARED THIS FOR YOU TODAY, TOO! ♡

ぱ
IT'S A SPIRIT BALL! ♡
FLASH
かっ
IT'S A SPECIAL ONE! ♡
HERE!
TAKE THIS AND GET BETTER!
HERE YOU GO! ♡
KYAHA!!
SHOVE
?!
MRPH!
NGH...
Nggghhh!
HEY!

GASP
...
HUH?
WHA ...?
SCRIB SCRIB SCRIB SCRIB SCRIB
CLATTER
MY CLASS-ROOM ...?
I FELL ASLEEP ?
WAS I DREAM-ING...?
?!
SERI-NUMA-SAN?
SCRIB SCRIB SCRIB
SCRIB SCRIB SCRIB
WHY IS SHE IN THE THIRD-YEAR CLASS-ROOM ?!

UH, WHAT'S THE MATTER?
A-ARE YOU OKAY...?
WHAT ARE YOU DOING?
FWIP
THIS IS...

BOOM
...A MAGIC CIRCLE.

HUH? SERI-NUMA-SAN...?
STAND
JOLT
OKAY! NOW IT SHOULD WORK!!
HERE I GO!

COME BACK!
ASUMA MUTSUMI !!
CLAP
WHA ...?
TH...THE CLUB-ROOM ?!
CLATTER
WHY ?!
GASP

BADUMP
ドキ…
UH... DID I FALL ASLEEP?
WHOA! I HAD SO MANY CRAZY DREAMS ...
I HOPE I DIDN'T SNORE.
FWIP
スッ…
SERI-NUMA-SAN?

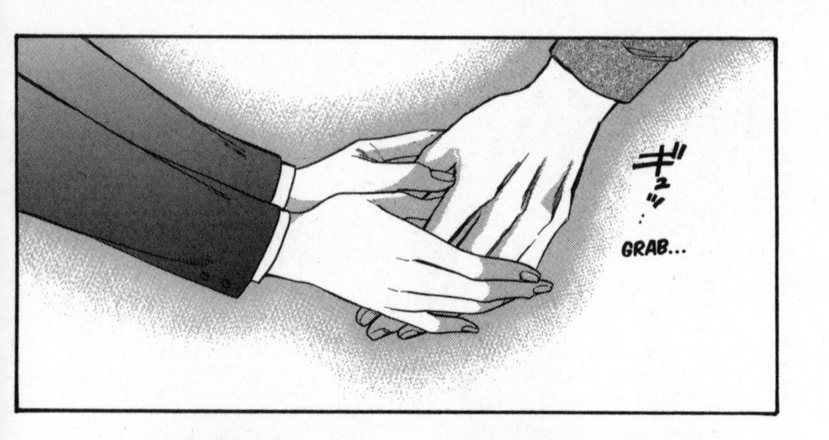
ギュッ
GRAB...

HUH?
SERI-
NUMA-
SAN...?
?!
?
WHAT'S
GOING
ON?
HER
HANDS
...
...FEEL
FAINT
TO THE
TOUCH
...
MUTSUMI-
SENPAI.

CAN YOU...
...HEAR MY VOICE ...?

HUH ...?
ER...
YEAH ...
OF COURSE I CAN HEAR YOUR VOICE.

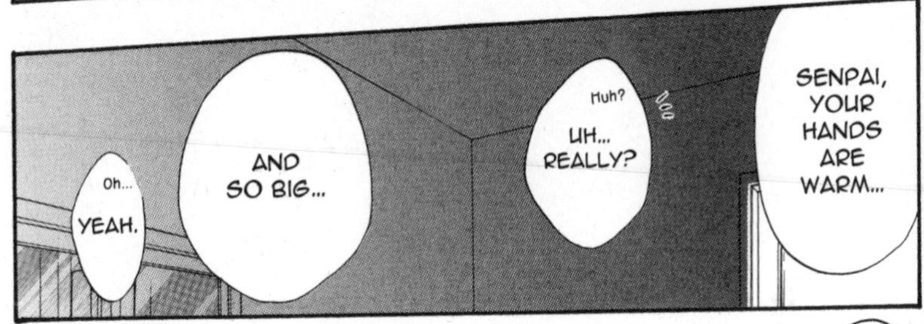

SENPAI, YOUR HANDS ARE WARM...
Huh?
UH... REALLY?
AND SO BIG...
Oh...
YEAH.

COME TO THINK OF IT...

THE FIRST TIME WE HELD HANDS WAS WHEN WE ENTERED THAT CAVE, HUH?

YEAH... THAT'S RIGHT.

YEAH,... I DIDN'T KNOW YOU WERE AFRAID OF THE DARK...

...AND YET YOU WANTED TO GO TO A PLACE LIKE THAT...

HA! HA! HA!

I GUESS YOU CAN SAY MY CURIOSITY WON OVER...

YOU'RE A STRANGE ONE, SENPAI.
HUH?
AND WHEN I SUDDENLY BECAME SKINNY, YOU RECOGNIZED ME RIGHT AWAY AND YOU TREATED ME THE SAME WAY YOU ALWAYS DID, HUH?
WELL, YOU WERE THE SAME PERSON INSIDE, SO...
YOU TOLD ME, "YOU'RE STILL YOU." WHEN YOU SAID THAT... YOU MADE ME FEEL SO AT EASE.

AND I REALLY ENJOYED OUR STROLL THROUGH TOWN...
YEAH. ME, TOO.
WE STILL HAVE TO FULFILL THAT PROMISE TO VISIT ANOTHER PLACE, HUH?
IN SPITE OF MY INDECISION... YOU TOLD ME THAT YOU'D CONTINUE...
...TO WAIT FOR ME...
SERI-NUMA-SAN?
YEAH.
WHERE SHALL WE GO NEXT?
YOU'VE ALWAYS BEEN BY MY SIDE...
AND...
EVEN WHEN I CAUSED YOU TROUBLE... YOU ALWAYS HELPED ME...

DRIP
DRIP
SERI-NUMA-SAN?
WHAT'S WRONG? WHY ARE YOU CRYING?
GRIP...
I'M WAITING ...
I'M WAITING, SO...

PLEASE
...
COME
BACK...

...
S...
SEN...
SENPAI ...?!
C...
CAN YOU HEAR ME?
CAN YOU UNDER-STAND WHAT I'M SAYING?
MUTSUMI-SENPAI!!
...
Y...
CLENCH
IT'S REALLY YOU...
YOU'RE SO WARM...

SHENPAIIII !!!
WAHHHHH!!
THANK GOD!!!
ぎゅう ぎゅう
SQUEEZE SQUEEZE
HEY!
OW! OW! OW! OW!

ブブブ
VMMM
CLATTER
CLATTER
CLATTER
CLATTER

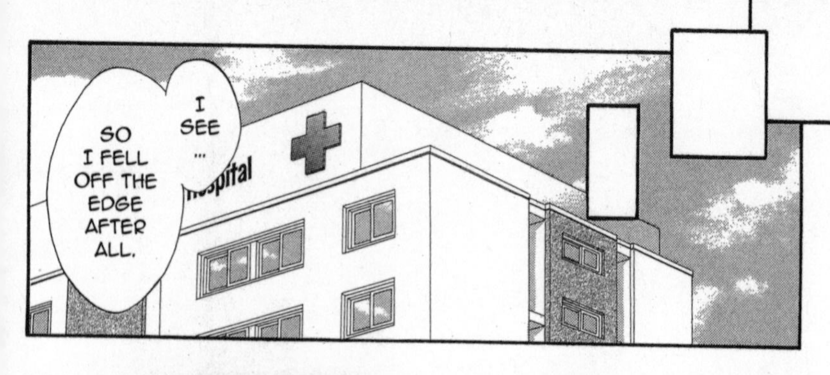
I SEE ...
SO I FELL OFF THE EDGE AFTER ALL.
Hospital

APPARENTLY YOU CAN LOSE YOUR MEMORY WHEN YOU HIT YOUR HEAD, SO...
IT'S UNDERSTANDABLE THAT YOU DON'T REMEMBER ANYTHING.
WELL ...
SINCE I WAS RESCUED AND MITSUBOSHI-KUN'S OKAY, IT LOOKS LIKE EVERYTHING IS ALL RIGHT.
N...NO IT'S NOT!!
JOLT

HOW COULD YOU DO SOMETHING SO RECKLESS?!
WELL, I CAN'T JUST SIT BY AND WATCH SOMEONE ABOUT TO FALL.
GOOD GRIEF!! YOU'RE ALWAYS THINKING ABOUT OTHER PEOPLE, SENPAI!!
IT WASN'T JUST THAT.
I DIDN'T WANT TO SEE YOU CRY, SERINUMA-SAN.
WHOOSH
HUH ...?!

YOU'D CRY IF SOMETHING AWFUL WERE TO HAPPEN TO YOUR CHILDHOOD FRIEND, WOULDN'T YOU, SERINUMA-SAN?
BADUMP

I'M IN LOVE WITH YOU.

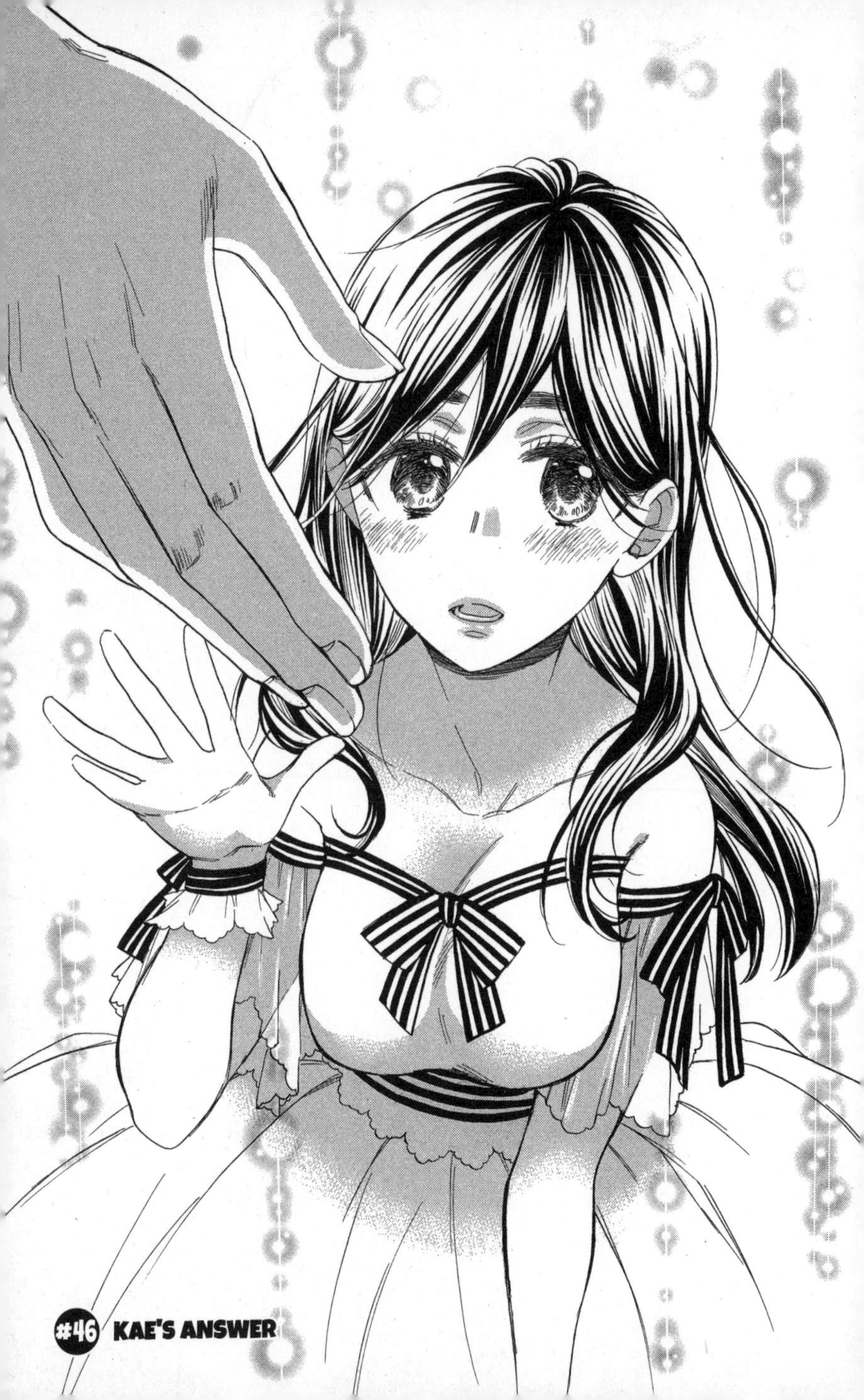
#46 KAE'S ANSWER

KISS HIM, NOT ME!

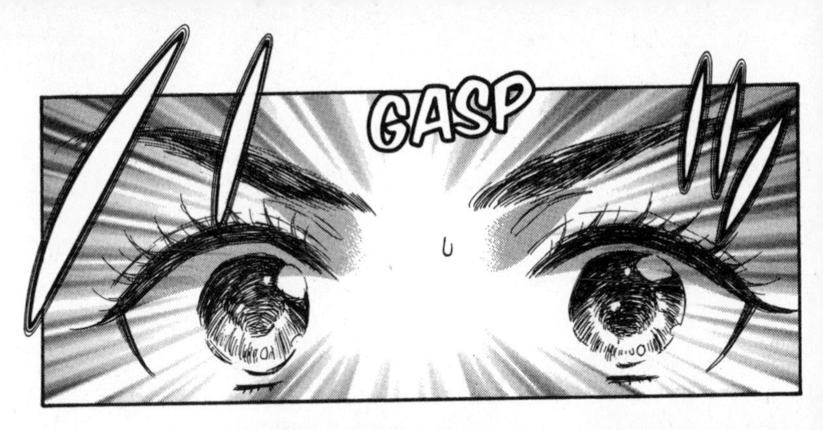
GASP

????
WH-WHAT DID I... JUST...?
LO...?
LAB? LOFT?
YOU KNOW ...
I HAD A WHOLE BUNCH OF DREAMS.

OH?
D-DREAMS?! REALLY?
TURN
YEAH.
DO YOU... REMEMBER WHEN WE FIRST MET LONG AGO ...
SERI-NUMA-SAN?

OF COURSE I DO!
WE RECRUITED MEMBERS FOR THE HISTORY CLUB, RIGHT?!
THOSE WERE GOOD TIMES!
HEH HEH HEH...
YEAH ...
WELL, ABOUT THAT!
BACK THEN...
I REMEMBER...
...THINKING THAT YOU WERE LIKE A BALL OF SUNSHINE.
ドキッ
BADUMP
HUH ...?!

A...
B-B-BALL OF SUNSHINE? I'VE BEEN TOLD THAT I'M LIKE A BALL OF MOCHI, BUT...
HA HA HA HA HA!
HEH HEH HEH
...
AND AFTER THAT, YOU FED ME A SPIRIT BALL!
IS THAT S...
HUH ?!
A...A SPIRIT BALL?!
AND AFTER THAT, YOU DREW A TRANS-MUTATION CIRCLE AND DID SOMETHING WITH IT!
?!
H...HOW DO YOU KNOW THAT...?
Oh my god...
HUH?
I...I ACTUALLY DID BOTH OF THOSE THINGS!!
WHA?!
THE SPIRIT BALL AND THE TRANS-MUTATION CIRCLE!!
I DID A BUNCH OF STUFF SO THAT YOU'D WAKE UP QUICKLY, SENPAI...
SO THOSE THINGS GOT THROUGH TO YOU ...!

HUH?
R... REALLY?
CRAZY ...!

WE TALKED ABOUT A BUNCH OF STUFF, TOO!!
YEAH, THAT'S RIGHT.
LIKE HOW WE WENT TO THAT CAVE...
YEAH!! EXACTLY!!
AMAZING! YOU WERE ABLE TO GET ALL THAT!!

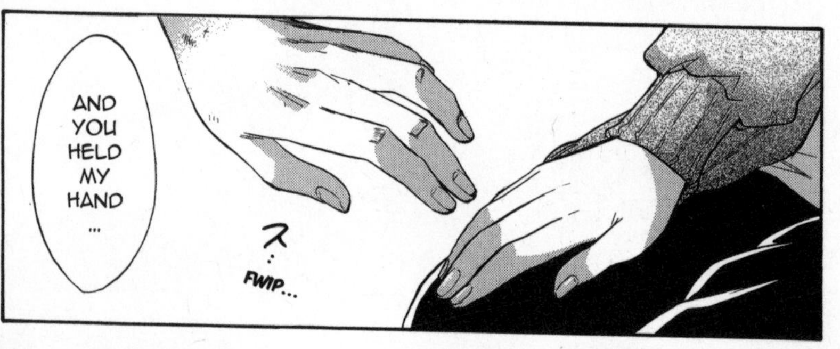
AND YOU HELD MY HAND ...
ス
FWIP...

ドキ
BADUMP
ぎゅっ
SQUEEZE
...LIKE THIS...

AND YOU TOLD ME TO COME BACK ...
AND THEN ...

GASP

...
HUH?
BADUMP
UH...
BADUMP
...
BADUMP
BADUMP
BADUMP
BADUMP
BADUMP
BADUMP

ガラッ
RAT
TLE
YO!
HOW'S IT GOING?

UH, SO SORRY!
I'll be on my way!
AHHH!! WAIT, ONIISAN!!

UH, I'M GONNA GO HOME TODAY!!
HUHHH? IT'S OKAY! TAKE ALL THE TIME YOU WANT.
NO, NO! DON'T BE SILLY!
TAKE CARE!!
ZOOM
AH!

SHE LEFT...
はっ
GASP
ニコ
GRIN
ニコ
GRIN

WHAT ...?
HUH? I'M JUST HAPPY TO SEE MY LITTLE BROTHER DOING WELL!
キャー!
SQUEAL
...

WAS THAT...?

A FEW DAYS LATER ...
ぼっ
ZED
え〜
DA
...EY...
HEY...
PAT
ぽんっ
HEY! SERINUMA !!
HUH?
はっ
GASP
WHAT'S WRONG? I WAS CALLING YOU OVER AND OVER...
OH, SORRY!

WHAT'S THE MATTER? ARE YOU TIRED?
ER...
STARE...
NANA-SHIMA-KUN...
WH-WHAT?
DO YOU HAVE A MOMENT?
HUH?
SQUEEZE
?!
SQUEEZE
SQUEEZE

ぱっ
RELEASE

OKAY ... THANKS.
YEAH...

UH... SURE THING...
どきどき
BADUMP BADUMP
...?
BADUMP BADUMP
どきどき
CHATTER
CHATTER

OH!
SERI-NUMA-SENPAI! GOOD MORNING.
GOOD MORNING, SHINO-MIYA-KUN.
WHAT BRINGS YOU TO THE FIRST-YEARS' SECTION OF THE SCHOOL ...?
SQUEEZE
?!
SQUEEZE SQUEEZE
OKAY ...

THANKS.
TMP
すたすた
TMP
?
?
WH... WHAT?
1-F
SERI-NUMA-SENPAI!
SHIMA-CHAN.
WHAT'S THE OCCASION, COMING ALL THE WAY TO MY CLASS...?
OH! DID YOU COME HERE TO SEE ME, BY ANY CHANCE?!

I'M SO GLAD!
Or is that wishful thinking?
YEAH.
NOD
HUH?
SQUEEZE
ぎゅっ！
?!
SQUEEZE
SQUEEZE
OKAY ...
WHAT DID SHE MEAN BY "OKAY" ...?
THANKS.
TMP
すた
TMP
すた
TMP
すた
BADUMP
BADUMP

IGA-RASHI-KUN...
LET'S SHAKE HANDS ...
CAN YOU...
...DO IT LIKE YOU ALWAYS DO?
HUH...?
UH, YEAH.
SURE.
OKAY, TODAY'S HAND-SHAKE...
SQUEEZE...
ぎゅっ..

OKAY...
DING
DONG
OH!
THE TEACHER'S COMING.
DANG
DONG
LET'S GET TO CLASS.
Oh.
AND THANKS!

CHATTER
CHATTER
TMP
TMP
TMP
CLENCH

DING
DONG
SERI-NUMA! LET'S GRAB LUNCH!
I'm starved!
CHATTER
CHATTER
Let's buy some bread!
OH, I GOTTA USE THE REST-ROOM!
YOU GO ON AHEAD!
SPLISH
SPLISH
FSHAAA
FSHAAA
SQUEAK
SURE ENOUGH ...
EVEN WHEN I TOUCHED EVERY-ONE ELSE'S HANDS...
PLIP...
...IT DIDN'T FEEL THE WAY THAT IT DID WITH MUTSUMI-SENPAI...

SLAM
バタン
TMP
たたた
TMP
TMP
ONLY SENPAI ...
ぽ
PAT
んっ
SERI-NUMA-SAN!

EEEEK!!
BAM!!
BOING
S... SERI-NUMA-SAN?!
THUD

WH... WHAT JUST HAP-PENED?! ARE YOU OKAY? ARE YOU HURT?
FWIP
I-I-IT'S NOTHING! I'M FINE...
S-SENPAI, YOU WERE ABLE TO COME TO SCHOOL!
YEAH, I JUST CAME NOW.
I-I'M GLAD!
ONLY SENPAI...

UDON
!!
MU-TSUMI-SENPAI?!
HEY, GUYS!!
YOU MUST'VE ALL BEEN REALLY WORRIED.
YAY
THANK GOD!!
You came back!
WEL-COME BACK!!
SOB!!
CHATTER
CHATTER

I KNOW NOW...
I KNOW ...
SEN-PAI...
SO...
ギュッ
CLENCH

THERE'S SOME-THING...
...I NOW HAVE TO DO.

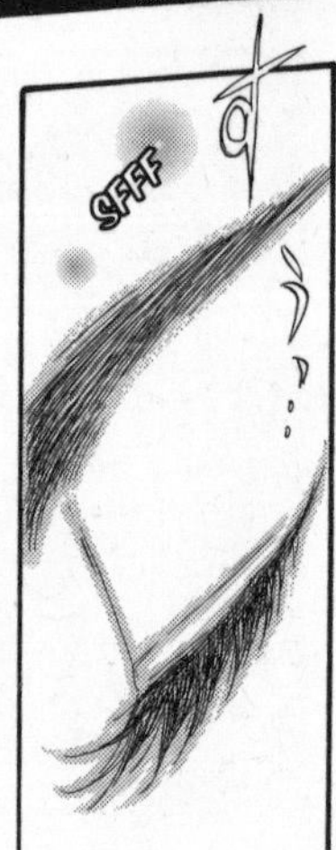
SFFF

TAP
I'd appreciate it.

Frequent (6)
OK
Read (5)
Today
Kae Serinuma
There's something I need to talk with you about. Can you come to the rooftop after school? I'd appreciate it.

VMMM

ガチャ
KER-CHAK

BEFORE, WHEN...
...YOU ALL CONFESSED YOUR FEELINGS TO ME...
I TOOK ADVANTAGE OF YOUR KINDNESS AND MADE ALL OF YOU WAIT FOR MY ANSWER...
BUT...
...I FINALLY REALIZED WHAT IT IS.

TO THINK IT TOOK ALL OF THIS FOR ME TO GET IT...
I HATE HOW CLUELESS I WAS, BUT...
...I FINALLY KNOW NOW.

I...

...LOVE
MUTSUMI-
SENPAI.

SO...
IGA-RASHI-KUN...
NANA-SHIMA-KUN...
SHINO-MIYA-KUN...
SHIMA-CHAN...
I'M SO SORRY...

MM...

UH-
HUH.

YEAH...

OKAY.
THANKS FOR GIVING US YOUR ANSWER.

STEP
ザッ
THUMP
どんっ
TAP
トッ
...
ぽかっ
WHAP
ぽかっ
WHAP
HEY!
PAT
TIME TO MAN UP!

バタン
SLAM

...
UM...!!
Y...
YES?

I...
...HAVE FEELINGS FOR YOU, MUTSUMI-SENPAI.
I LOVE YOU...!!
I...
S... SENPAI...
WILL YOU...
...BE MY BOY-FRIEND?
IF IT'S ALL RIGHT ...
...WITH YOU...

YANK
HUG

GLADLY.
I LOVE YOU, TOO.

I NEVER THOUGHT THE DAY WOULD COME THAT I'D BE...
...THE PRINCESS IN THE ARMS OF HER PRINCE.

#47 CAN WE MAKE OUR RELATIONSHIP WORK?

KiSS HiM, NOT ME!

MP
CHO
TASTY?
YEAH!
HAVE SOME TOO, SERI-NUMA-SAN!
MUNCH もぐ MUNCH もぐ
きゃっ SQUEAL ♡
HERE!
OPEN WIIIDE! ♡

UH...
Gross...

WE'RE GONNA MOVE TO ANOTHER SEAT...
Ehh...
WE'RE GETTING IN YOUR WAY...
HUH ?!
WHY ?!

LET'S AT LEAST HAVE LUNCH TOGETHER!
BUT...
Uh...
YEAH! YOU'RE NOT IN THE WAY AT ALL ...
OH!

YOU HAVE SOME RICE ON YOUR CHEEK, SENPAI!
HUH? REALLY?
HA! HA! HA!
SO ANNOYING!!
OH GOSH! HERE! LET ME!
TEE HEE HEE!
OH! THANK YOU!

UGH...
THEY'RE SO CLUELESS THAT IT CAN'T BE FOR REAL!!
S..SUCH AN AWFUL THING TO DO IN FRONT OF THE PEOPLE WHO WERE REJECTED..
Be strong!
AND YOU KNOW WHAT?!
MUTSUMI-SENPAI COMES TO OUR CLASS...
ARGH!
しわっ
...EVERY BREAK!!
YEAH, THAT'S RIGHT.
R... REALLY?!
AND ON TOP OF THAT...

ばんっ
BOOM

UM... UH...
CUDDLE
NUZZLE
WHISPER
WHISPER
WHISPER
WHISPER
WHAT'S UP, IGARASHI-KUN?
WELL...
GLARE
COULD YOU NOT BE ALL LOVEY-DOVEY IN FRONT OF US REJECTED FOLK?!
AT LEAST DON'T DO IT HERE!!

HUH?!
WHAT DO YOU MEAN "LOVEY-DOVEY" ...?
EEK!
HOW MUCH MORE LOVEY-DOVEY CAN YOU GET ?!
YOU CAN'T POSSIBLY BE SERIOUS!

WELL... OUR BODIES JUST END UP GETTING LIKE THIS.

I DON'T WANT TO BE APART FROM YOU...
...FOR EVEN JUST A LITTLE WHILE.
SWOOON
SH... SHENPAI! ♡
MURMUR

NGH... IT'S JUST TOO MUCH...
NNGH...
I STILL HAVEN'T GOTTEN OVER THE HURT, Y'KNOW!
I FEEL YOU, SENPAI...
JUST THINKING ABOUT IT BRINGS ME TO TEARS!!
NOD NOD
TEAR

YOU UNDER-STAND ME, DON'T YOU, SHINO-MIYAAA?!
GRAB
I DO! I REALLY DO!!
SNAP
SNAP
NOD NOD

...

HUH? NANASHIMA-KUN?

WELL, YEAH... IT'S NOT JUST NANA...
MURMUR
TO BE HONEST, IT'S TOUGH FOR ME, TOO...AS PATHETIC AS IT IS...
MURMUR

GASP
O... OH...
I'M SORRY. I HAD NO IDEA!

OKAY, WHAT SHOULD WE DO, SERINUMA-SAN?
CUDDLE CUDDLE
HMMM... I DON'T KNOW. WHAT DO YOU THINK, SENPAI?
ANNOYED
OH!! I KNOW! NEXT TIME, I'LL GO TO YOU, SENPAI!
BRILLIANT IDEA!!
HUH? YOU'D DO THAT?
YEAH!!
I'LL GO SEE YOU... ♡
SERINUMA-SAN...! THAT MAKES ME SO HAPPY! ♡
URK!
SO ANNOYING!!
AW! WHAT A SURPRISE!
TO THINK KAE-CHAN WOULD BE SO BLINDLY IN LOVE WITH SOMEONE!!
PEEK
Uh... NAKANO-SAN...

Selected Pictures
FWIP
FWIP
WELL... IT MIGHT ALSO BE 'CAUSE OF WHAT HAPPENED TO AKANE!
HM? WHAT ARE YOU DOING, KAE-CHAN?
HUH? OH, I'M JUST DELETING PICS THAT I DON'T NEED...
"DON'T NEED" ...?
ISN'T THAT AKANE?
YOU'RE OKAY WITH THAT?
AKANE? WHO'S AKANE?
HUH?

RUMBLE
RUMBLE
RUMBLE
RUMBLE
I HAVE NO INTEREST IN A GUY WHO BETRAYS MASTER FOR A GIRL AND THEN HAS THE GALL TO MAKE BABIES WITH HER.
RUMBLE
RUMBLE
RUMBLE

TRAITOR TRAITOR TRAITOR TRAITOR TRAITOR TRAITOR TRAITOR TRAITOR TRAITOR
WH... WHOA...

SO... ALL HER PASSION FOR AKANE MIGHT'VE TRANS-FERRED OVER TO MUTSUMI-SENPAI, HUH...
I...I SEE...
So it has nothing to do with Mitsu-boshi...
STILL ...
HOW ANNOY-ING...
うっとり
LOVESICK
The next day...
3-C
ひょいっ
PEEK
SENPAI! ♡
SERI-NUMA-SAN!

GOOD MORNING! IT'S BEEN A DAY SINCE WE LAST SAW EACH OTHER...!
MURMUR
I MISSED YOU...
SERI-NUMA-SAN...
HEY... IS SHE ...?
MU-TSUMI OF ALL PEOPLE, ACTING LIKE THAT ...?
HIS GIRL-FRIEND ?
MURMUR
MURMUR
NO WAY...
I MISSED YOU, TOO!
SH... SHENPAI!
SWOON
SWOON
UH...
THEY CAN'T KEEP THEIR HANDS OFF EACH OTHER!!
WHAT'S UP WITH THOSE TWO...?!

TMP...
MUTSUMI ...

YASHIRO-KUN...
IS SHE YOUR GIRL-FRIEND, BY ANY CHANCE?
ADJUST
くいっ
NICE SMILE
YEAH !!
SENPAI, WHO IS THIS PERSON ...?

SQUEE
HE'S MY CLASS-MATE, YA-SHIRO-KUN.
HE'S THE CAPTAIN OF THE SHOGI CLUB, AND WE OCCA-SIONALLY PLAY TOGETHER.
OH, I SEE! PLEASED TO MEET YOU!
THAT'S RIGHT! I'M SERINUMA! I'M A KOHAI FROM THE HISTORY CLUB...
ARE YOU A SECOND-YEAR STUDENT?
I'M MUTSUMI-SENPAI'S GIRLFRIEND. ♡
I SEE. IT'S A PLEA-SURE.
BOW
BOW
BOW
LIKE-WIIISE! ♡
The pleasure's all mine!
OH! YIKES!
DING
DONG
DANG
DONG
THE MOR-NING PERIOD IS SO SHORT!
I... I'LL BE BACK!
TAKE CARE ON YOUR WAY BACK!
I WILL!
SHE'S CUTE.

OH... YEAH.
I KNOW!
NOT JUST THAT ...
SHE'S A REALLY GOOD GIRL.
HM...
Bye-bye!
Take care!
See you tomorrow!
CHIME

OH! IT'S GRANDPA!
Gramps
Today
A new one!
HE'S DOING COSPLAY AGAIN!
Ha! Ha! Ha!
Whoa! HE IS!
AH!! EVEN GRANDMA'S DOING IT!!
SERINUMA-SAN, YOUR GRANDPARENTS ARE SUCH FUN PEOPLE!
I MET THEM ONCE, RIGHT?
I DON'T KNOW WHETHER THEY'RE INTERESTING OR JUST WEIRD, BUT THEY'RE ALWAYS HAVING FUN!
WOW! SOUNDS NICE.
HEH! HEH!
SPEAKING OF WHICH, WHAT ARE YOUR GRANDPARENTS LIKE, SENPAI?
MY GRANDPARENTS ON MY DAD'S SIDE LIVE IN THE NORTH, AND THEY'RE DOING WELL.
MY GRANDPA ON MY MOM'S SIDE PASSED AWAY WHEN I WAS IN JUNIOR HIGH.
I WAS REALLY CLOSE WITH MY GRANDPA, SO IT CAME AS A SHOCK WHEN HE DIED.
MY GRANDPA WAS THE ONE WHO GOT ME INTO HISTORY AND TAUGHT ME SHOGI.

I...I SEE...
I'M SORRY, I...
OH! NOT AT ALL! DON'T BE!
BUT ...
HE WAS A VERY IMPORTANT PERSON TO YOU, RIGHT, SENPAI?
I WISH I COULD'VE MET HIM ...
YEAH.
THE 16TH IS THE MONTHIVERSARY OF HIS DEATH... WOULD YOU LIKE TO VISIT HIS GRAVE WITH ME?
HUH?
I WANT TO INTRO-DUCE YOU TO HIM.

AND TELL HIM HOW PRECIOUS YOU ARE TO ME.
...
O...OF COURSE! I'D BE HAPPY TO!
FOR SURE!!
REALLY? THANK YOU!
SQUEAL
SQUEAL

...
AND SO...
SENPAIIII!
INTIMATE AND HAPPY, THE TWO SEEMED ON TRACK TO DEEPEN THEIR RELATION-SHIP...
(WHILE EARNING THE DISAP-PROVAL OF THOSE AROUND THEM...)
D...Dis***?
HOW-EVER!!
GOSH! I TOLD HIM "GOOD NIGHT" ALREADY!
BUT SENPAI WON'T STOP SENDING ME MES-SAGES!
Heh heh heh heh!
OH DEAR!
TA-DAH!

...
HUH...?
IT WAS THEN...

MIRAGE SAGA
SEQUEL ANNOUNCED!!!
...THAT SHE WAS REMINDED...
...OF WHO SHE WAS!!

The following day...
SHIMA-SHIMA-SHIMA-SHIMA-SHIMA-SHIMA-SHIMA-...
THUD THUD THUD
THUD
THUD
THUD
SHIMA-SHIMA-SHIMA-SHIMA-SHIMA-SHIMA-CHAAAN!!
DID YOU SEE IT?!
BOOM
I DID!!
OH MY GOD! THAT SILHOUETTE OF THE SWORD AT THE END OF THE TEASER! TH...TH... TH...TH... THAT WAS SHION'S SWORD, RIGHT?!
ABSOLUTELY!!
THE CHIPPED END OF THE SWORD... THAT WAS DEFINITELY SHION'S!!
S-SO THEN... THE FACT THAT THAT WAS PUT IN THERE...
*Super fast talking
AHHHHH!!

EEEEEEKK!
AHHHH!
I HEAR SERI-NUMA-SENPAI SCREAM-ING...
WHAT'S THE MATTER ?!
DASH
IT'S HERE !!!

IT'S CRAZY, SHINO-MIYA-KUUUN!
SHAKE SHAKE SHAKE SHAKE SHAKE
SHION MIGHT COME BACK TO LIFE, SHINO-MIYA-KUUUN !!
HUH?
ACK!
SHAKE SHAKE
STOP!
NOT JUST THAT!! THEY'RE HAVING A FIRST SEASON RETRO-SPECTIVE URGENT MEETING !!
YOU'RE OBVI-OUSLY GOING, RIGHT, SENPAI ?!
OF COURSE! I'M GONNA GET A TICKET OR DIE TRYING! UH, SO IT'S NEXT MONTH ON THE...
THE 16TH!!
PAUSE
...THE 16TH?
THE 16TH, HUH ?!

DING
DONG
SEN... PAI...
STAGGER
STAGGER
OH, HEY, SERI-NUMA-SAN...
WHAT'S UP?

BOOM
I'M SOOO SORRY!!
?!
HUH?! WHAT'S THE MATTER?!

TH... THE TRUTH IS...
THE MIRAGE SAGA SEQUEL HAS BEEN ANNOUNCED, AND...AND...
SHION... SHION MIGHT COME BACK TO LIFE!!
HUH? SHION-SAN? REALLY?
THAT'S GREAT!!
UH...
Angel

PRICKLE PRICKLE
UGH... THE GUILT I'M FEELING...
S...
SO...
THERE'S AN EVENT... AND...
IT'S ON THE 16TH OF NEXT MONTH...!

THE 16TH...

OH!
B-B-B-B-BUT IT'S IN TWO PARTS, AND THE FIRST PART STARTS IN THE EARLY AFTERNOON!
FWIP
S...SO WOULD IT BE OKAY WITH YOU... IF WE MET AFTER THAT'S DONE?!

UH... WELL, DO YOU WANT TO MEET IN THE MORNING, THEN?

I HAVE TO LINE UP FOR MERCH IN THE MORNING!!

I'M SOOOO SORRYYYY!

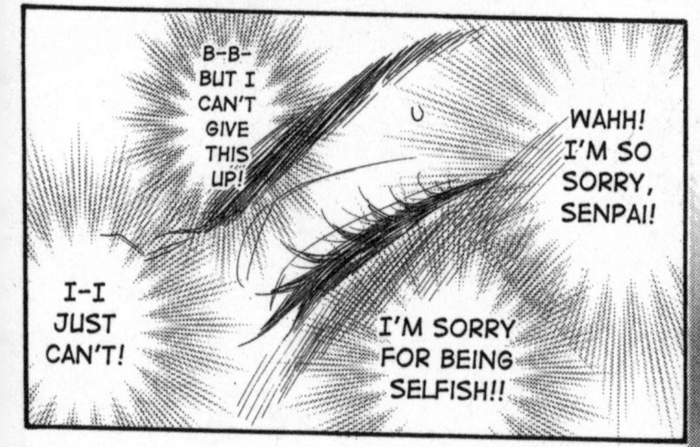
WAHH! I'M SO SORRY, SENPAI!
B-B-BUT I CAN'T GIVE THIS UP!
I'M SORRY FOR BEING SELFISH!!
I-I JUST CAN'T!

PAT ぽん
WHEN DOES THE EVENT END?
HUH?
UH, THE EVENT'S UNTIL THREE.
IT'S OKAY, THEN.
GO HAVE FUN.
BESIDES, IT'S SOMETHING YOU LOVE, SERINUMA-SAN.
SWOOON
SH...
SHENPAIII! THANK YOU SOOO MUCH! I WUV YOUUUU!! ♡♡♡
WHOA!
There it is...
She "wuvs" him...

MUTSUMI-SENPAI IS SO KIND...
HE REALLY UNDER-STANDS ME...♡
HE ACCEPTS EVERYTHING I DO...

HEH HEH...
I'M GLAD YOU'RE GONNA HAVE FUN.
...

HOW-EVER ...
BLAH へらへら BLAH へらへら BLAH へらへら BLAH へらへら

EEEK!
Yummy!
...

On another day
I HAVE TO HELP SHIMA-CHAN WITH HER DEADLINE! I'M SOOO SORRY!!
The "Mirage-Saga" book is coming out, so I wanna help her so badly!
OKAY.

And on another day
OH!
AND SO...
IS THAT SO?
Checking her Twitter
UH-HUH ?

And on yet another day
Kae Serinuma
Sorry! They're showing a season one marathon on Neko-Neko!
SORRY

YOUR GIRLFRIEND HASN'T BEEN AROUND THESE DAYS.
TAK
SHE'S APPARENTLY BUSY.

SERI-NUMA'S COMPLETELY RETURNED TO THE WAY SHE WAS...
WELL... THAT'S HOW SHE WAS ORIGINALLY.
Fresh Orange
I'd forgotten about that these days...
YEAH... BUT STILL...

ARE YOU OKAY, MUTSUMI-SENPAI...?
UH...
I mean, y'know...
HUH? WHAT DO YOU MEAN?
WHA?
SMILE!
SERINUMA-SAN SEEMS TO BE HAVING FUN, SO I'M HAPPY FOR HER!

WHAAAA?! HE'S SO UNDER-STANDING ...!!

INCRE-DIBLE... HE REALLY IS SOME-THING ELSE!
If it were me, I'd be really pissed...
YEAH ...
HE'S LIKE THE BUDDHA ...

MU-TSUMI?
IS SOME-THING THE MATTER?
HUH? WHAT?
YOU SEEM DOWN...
HUH...?

HUH? ME...?
NO-THING'S THE MATTER ...
REALLY ?
サイコホール
Saiko Hall
On the day of the event ...
TAKE CARE, SENPAI!
I'LL BE STICKING AROUND FOR THE SECOND PART OF THE EVENT!
ザワ
CHATTER
Urgent Meeting
Staff Only
ザワ
CHATTER

OKAY, SEE YA!!
CHATTER
I CAN'T BELIEVE IT WENT 20 MINUTES OVER ...
GASP!
AND THERE WAS A SUPER LONG LINE TO THE REST-ROOMS ...
AHH! THIS IS BAD!!
TMP
TMP
TMP
CHATTER
CHATTER
OHH, BUT IT WAS SOOO FUN!!
THE SELECTED SCREENINGS FOR THE FIRST SEASON RETRO-SPECTIVE, AND THE INSIDER COMMEN-TARY!!
THEY TALKED ABOUT ALL SORTS OF JUICY STUFF!
I BET THE SECOND PART IS GOING TO BE EVEN MORE AWESOME!!
AHHH! I WISH I COULD BE THERE!!
PANT
PANT
PANT
PANT
PANT
PANT
THAT'S RIGHT! I HAVE TO CONTACT SENPAI FIRST!!
ACK! NO, I CAN'T !!
UHH...
YOU THERE.
HUH?

HI.
HUH ?!
Y... YOU'RE MUTSUMI-SENPAI'S ...?! UHH...
IT'S YA-SHIRO.
YOU CAME TO THE EVENT, TOO, HUH?
Y-YES !!
HUH ?
UM...
YA-SHIRO-SENPAI, ARE YOU ALSO ...?!
ME?
SST
OF COURSE.
MIRAGE SAGA IS THE BEST ANIME EVER...!!
BOOM
WOW!! INCRED-IBLE!!
UU

SO YOU'RE A FEL-LOW FAN!!
YES, IT SEEMS SO.
AND WASN'T THAT EVENT JUST THE BEST?
YES! IT WAS SO MUCH FUN!!
SQUEAL SQUEAL
HEH HEH HEH

YOU AREN'T GOING TO THE SECOND PART?
HUH?

I, uh...
I HAVE SOME-THING I NEED TO DO, SO...
Heh heh heh.
THE TRUTH IS...
THE FRIEND I WAS SUPPOSED TO GO WITH SUDDENLY COULDN'T MAKE IT, SO...
...I HAVE A SPARE TICKET...
HUH ?!
A SPARE TICKET ...?!
AGH!
IT'S SUCH A SHAME FOR THE SEAT TO BE EMPTY ...
SST...
OH, WELL.
MIRAGE SAGA URGENT MEETING!!
ROW A SEAT 12
A12
GASP
NO, I CAN'T!!
UH, UM!
TH-THAT'S REALLY TOO BAD!!

THE SEAT'S AT THE VERY FRONT...

ROW A SEAT 12

...AND RIGHT AT THE CENTER!!

LATER ON, KAE SERI-NUMA SAID...

..."I HAVE NO MEMORY OF WHAT HAPPENED AFTER..."

TO BE CONTINUED
IN VOLUME 13 OF

KISS HIM,
NOT ME!

I HAD INTENDED TO MAKE MITSUBOSHI A MORE COMICAL CHARACTER. BUT AS HIS CHARACTER CHANGED, I DECIDED TO TAKE HIM AS FAR AS I COULD IN A DIFFERENT DIRECTION. I QUITE LIKE HIM, AS HE BRINGS A UNIQUE QUALITY TO THE STORY. HE'S ALSO A CHARACTER I WANT TO DEVELOP A BIT MORE. I HOPE TO REVISIT HIS CHARACTER SOMEDAY...
ALSO! FINALLY! KAE AND MUTSUMI ARE TOGETHER!
I TRIED FROM EARLY ON TO GET THESE TWO TOGETHER, BUT IT SEEMS A LOT OF PEOPLE WERE SURPRISED BY THE DEVELOPMENT. HA HA.
WHAT'LL HAPPEN WITH THE RELATIONSHIP OF THESE TWO SPACE CASES...?! AND LET'S NOT FORGET NISHINA, SHINOMIYA, IGARASHI, AND NANASHIMA...!! STICK AROUND WITH THIS GANG FOR JUST A BIT LONGER!
JUNKO
THANKS!
Special Adviser / EIKI EIKI-SENSEI
Staff / AKI-SAN, SHINOHARA-SAN, ROKKU-SAN, SHIROE-SAN, YUKI-SAN
#44, 45 Collaboration / S-SAMA

AUTHOR'S NOTE

WHEN WORKING ON THIS MANGA, I LEAVE A BUNCH OF ANIME AND FOREIGN DRAMAS ON WITHOUT REALLY PAYING CLOSE ATTENTION TO THEM.
BUT I KEEP COMING TO THE LAST PART OF A SERIES AND REALIZING THAT I'VE ALREADY WATCHED THAT PARTICULAR SHOW.
THIS ISN'T JUST AN ISSUE OF LACKING MEMORY...IT'S BEYOND THAT...

-JUNKO

Translation Notes

"She was collecting spirit balls.", page 24

Those familiar with the *Dragon Ball Z* series may recognize this as the process Goku goes through to collect his spirit bomb. The original term for this move is "*genki dama*" which directly translates to "*spirit ball*". Because it wouldn't make sense for a bomb to be used on Mustumi, the direct translation was used.

Masamune-sama and *Sengoku Basara*, page 51

Sengoku Basara is a series of fighting-action video games developed and published by Capcom. Its story is loosely based on the real events of the titular Sengoku era of feudal Japan, and its characters are fictionalized versions of some of the most predominant feudal lords and historical figures during that time. The "Masamune-sama" that Kae is referring to is Date Masamune, the then-ruler of the Date clan who later went on to become one of the most powerful daimyo in Japanese history, and who founded the modern-day city of Sendai.

"Castle Guard", page 54

This refers to the card game seen in Volume 5. Unfortunately, it was previously translated as *Castle Cards* when, as a parody of *Cardfight!! Vanguard*, it should've been translated as *Castle Guard*. In the anime, the game was called *Guard the Castle*.

"Ok, you punks! Let's party!!", page 55

In this scene, Kae is imitating her favorite character from the *Sengoku Basara* series, Date Masamune. In the Japanese version, Masamune is given a bad-boy character, acts like he's in a biker gang, and for some reason mixes English phrases like "Let's party!" into his regular speech.

"The 16th is the monthiversary of his death...", page 132

A death anniversary is a custom observed in several East Asian countries, including China, Korea, and Japan. Like a birthday, it is celebrated each year, but instead of on the date of birth of the individual being celebrated, it is celebrated on the day on which a family member or other significant individual passed away. Even though Mutsumi-senpai's grandfather passed away several years ago, he still honors the anniversary of his death, but instead of visiting him on only the day he died, he visits him every month on the day in which he died, which in this case is the 16th.

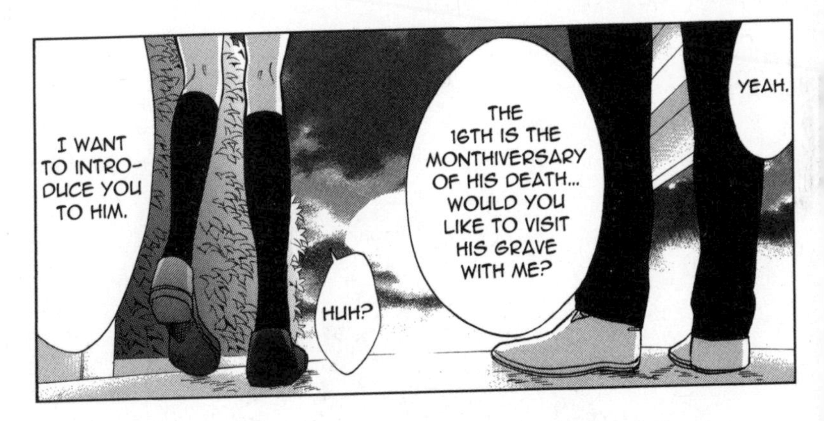

sweetness & lightning
By Gido Amagakure
KC
KODANSHA COMICS

Japan's most powerful spirit medium delves into the ghost world's greatest mysteries!

Story by Kyo Shirodaira, famed author of mystery fiction and creator of *Spiral*, *Blast of Tempest*, and *The Record of a Fallen Vampire*.

Both touched by spirits called yôkai, Kotoko and Kurô have gained unique superhuman powers. But to gain her powers Kotoko has given up an eye and a leg, and Kurô's personal life is in shambles. So when Kotoko suggests they team up to deal with renegades from the spirit world, Kurô doesn't have many other choices, but Kotoko might just have a few ulterior motives...

IN/SPECTRE

STORY BY KYO SHIRODAIRA
ART BY CHASHIBA KATASE

"An emotional and artistic tour de force! We see incredible triumph, and crushing defeat... each panel [is] a thrill!"
–Anitay
"A journey that's instantly compelling."
—Anime News Network
WELCOME TO THE BALLROOM
By Tomo Takeuchi

Kiss Hi . Names, characters,
places, thor's imagination or are
used fic nts, locales, or persons,
living o

A Koda

Kiss Hi Junko
English

Published in the United States by Kodansha Comics,
an imprint of Kodansha USA Publishing, LLC, New York.

Publication rights for this English edition arranged through Kodansha Ltd., Tokyo.

First published in Japan in 2017 by Kodansha Ltd., Tokyo, as *Watashi Ga Motete Dousunda* volume 12.

ISBN 978-1-63236-493-7

Printed in the United States of America.

www.kodanshacomics.com

9 8 7 6 5 4 3 2 1

Translation: David Rhie
Lettering: Jacqueline Wee
Editing: Ajani Oloye
Kodansha Comics edition cover design: Phil Balsman